CW00348321

Friends
are the family
we choose for ourselves

This edition published by Ravette Publishing 2006.

Printed and bound in Belgium

ISBN 10: 1-84161-254-5
ISBN 13: 978-1-84161-254-6

RR
RAVETTE PUBLISHING

When friends meet, hearts warm

Happiness is being married to your best friend

Candy floss

There are special people who touch our lives in a certain way and having known them, we will never be the same

For listening and
caring, for giving
and sharing,
for always being there,
thank you

A hug is a
great gift
one size fits all

Because we can't call people without wings angels, we call them friends

There's nothing better
than a good friend,
except a good friend
with chocolate

Good friends are
like angels,
you don't have to
see them to know
they are there

friends bring out the
beautiful things in each
other that nobody else
looks hard enough
to find

Not only do
I love you,
but you're my
best friend

You can't have
too many friends,
or pairs of
shoes.

Friends are the family we choose for ourselves

Friends like you don't grow on trees I know that this is true, but if friends were flowers there is no doubt how quickly I'd pick you

I can't imagine
in all the world
a better friend
than you

You'll always
be my
friend

...you know
too much

Some people make the world more special just by being in it

When I
count
my
blessings

I always
count you
twice

Precious

and few are

friends

like you

Other BORN TO SHOP titles available ...

	ISBN	Price
Another day in paradise	1 84161 255 3	£4.99
I never met a calorie I didn't like	1 84161 256 1	£4.99
All men are created equal ... equally useless	1 84161 257 X	£4.99

HOW TO ORDER   Please send a cheque/postal order in £ sterling, made payable to 'Ravette Publishing' for the cover price of the books and allow the following for post & packaging ...

UK & BFPO	70p for the first book & 40p per book thereafter
Europe & Eire	£1.30 for the first book & 70p per book thereafter
Rest of the world	£2.20 for the first book & £1.10 per book thereafter

RAVETTE PUBLISHING LTD
Unit 3 Tristar Centre
Star Road
Partridge Green
West Sussex RH13 8RA
Tel: 01403 711443 Fax: 01403 711554 Email: ravettepub@aol.com